936.14

SUSAN

D1580826

930.

BRONZE AGE
METALWORK

IN SOUTHERN BRITAIN

cirencester
college
a beacon college

Cover photograph
Gold ornament made from composite gold strip;
diameter 77 mm (3 inches);
from Yeovil (Somerset).
(Somerset County Museum.)

Published by
SHIRE PUBLICATIONS LTD
Cromwell House, Church Street, Princes Risborough,
Aylesbury, Bucks HP17 9AJ, UK.

Series Editor: James Dyer

ISBN 0 85263 680 6

First published 1984

Set in 11 point Times and printed in Great Britain by
C. I. Thomas & Sons (Haverfordwest) Ltd,
Press Buildings, Merlins Bridge, Haverfordwest, Dyfed.

Contents

Museums

This list gives those museums which have fairly large collections of metalwork and which usually have some of their collection on display. Much important material, however, is also held elsewhere.

Ashmolean Museum of Art and Archaeology, Beaumont Street, Oxford OX1 2PH. Telephone: Oxford (0865) 512651.

Brighton Art Gallery and Museum, Church Street, Brighton. Telephone: Brighton (0273) 603005.

British Museum, Great Russell Street, London WC1B 3DG. Telephone: 01-636 1555/8.

Castle Museum, Norwich NR1 3JU. Telephone: Norwich (0603) 611277 extension 279.

Dorset County Museum, High West Street, Dorchester, Dorset DT1 1XA. Telephone: Dorchester (0305) 62735.

Jewry Wall Museum of Archaeology, St Nicholas Circle, Leicester. Telephone: Leicester (0533) 554100 extension 217.

National Museum of Wales, Cathays Park, Cardiff CF1 3NP. Telephone: Cardiff (0222) 397951.

Pitt Rivers Museum, South Parks Road, Oxford OX1 3PP. Telephone: Oxford (0865) 512541.

Rougemont House Museum, Castle Street, Exeter. Telephone: Exeter (0392) 56724.

Royal Institution of Cornwall, County Museum, River Street, Truro, Cornwall. Telephone: Truro (0872) 2205.

Royal Pavilion, Brighton BN1 1UE. Telephone: Brighton (0273) 603005.

Salisbury and South Wiltshire Museum, The King's House, 65 The Close, Salisbury SP1 2EN. Telephone: Salisbury (0722) 332151.

Somerset County Museum, Taunton Castle, Castle Green, Taunton TA1 4AA. Telephone: Taunton (0823) 55504.

University Museum of Archaeology and Anthropology, Downing Street, Cambridge CB2 3DZ. Telephone: Cambridge (0223) 359714.

Wiltshire Archaeological and Natural History Society, Devizes Museum, 41 Long Street, Devizes, Wiltshire SN10 1NS. Telephone: Devizes (0380) 2765.

List of illustrations

1
Introduction

Approaches to the study of bronze age metalwork

Metalwork is one of the most important fossils which the bronze age has left to us and it is beautiful and exciting material, often very well preserved — indeed, in the case of gold, incomparably well preserved. We study it in order to learn more of the workings of bronze age society: this simple proposition is, however, more controversial than it appears.

Some approaches are universally accepted. *Typology*, the definition of forms and the comparison of one piece with another to create a ladder of typological development and hence of relative chronology across Britain and Europe, remains fundamental, in spite of its severe problems. The application of radiocarbon dates can peg the relative dating to real centuries, and this has resulted in a lengthening of the early bronze age and an updating of British phases to fit continental counterparts. *Metallurgical investigation*, still in its infancy, can tell us much about the smelting, casting and finishing processes used by ancient smiths. *Metal analysis*, laboratory techniques designed to demonstrate the precise chemical make-up of metal objects and ore samples, can throw light upon the nature of the alloys in use at various times and places, and on the sources of the constituent metals. The shifting sequence of trans-European trading patterns which this is revealing has enormous implications.

Apparently less reliant upon 'hard' evidence (although actually no more subjective than many of the conclusions of typology or even metal analysis) are efforts to *characterise* metalwork, to place all the multifarious types into broad categories of, say, weapons, ornaments, tools and scrap waiting for the melting pot. When this is done to the multiple metal finds, often in the past called 'hoards', which are one of the most striking phenomena of the bronze age and deserve further sympathetic attention, the resulting information has far reaching implications for our concept of changing bronze age society. The same is true of the *context* of metal: did it come from a barrow, a hut, a field system or the site of a later hillfort? Equally important is the *style* of the find: was it laid with the dead, or mixed with household rubbish and smithing debris, or buried in a box? And what do these differences mean, discernible despite the poor quality of early recording and similar problems?

Another dimension of the metalwork, whether in single or group finds, is the *distribution* of broadly contemporary material across the landscape. In spite of very serious difficulties concerning the size of the original populations and of differential discovery, distributional patterns sometimes force themselves to our notice, and, used cautiously, they can offer insights into settlement patterns and the exploitation of the landscape. All this, essentially, is to do with the role of metalwork in the social organisation of its day, and with the development of approaches which enable us to understand it better.

The history of the study of bronze age metalwork is long and complicated. In this book I have tried to express current views without lingering on controversies, but inevitably many important debates have been greatly simplified. I have tried to strike a balance between straight descriptions of the metal types and discussion of their implications. Regimented ranks of axes on a page of drawings, each with its cross-section, would be inappropriate in a book intended to introduce and encourage. I have, therefore, made the illustrations less rigid. Designations for both types and phases present a problem since so many systems are in current use. I have given an idea of the variants where possible, using names rather than numbers because they are easier to remember. I have given real, not radiocarbon, dates, but they should be read as broad indications.

This book is concerned with the metal industries of southern Britain, which I have defined as lying south of the Trent, although I have sometimes looked beyond this area for types to illustrate. Throughout the bronze age, the industries of southern Britain have a unified character which links them with those of north-western Europe and differentiates them from those of northern Britain and Ireland.

A book of this kind owes a great deal to those working in the field, and I have been particularly glad to draw upon the expertise of Dr Peter Northover. I am grateful to those many museum curators who have helped me, especially Dr Stuart Needham, Elizabeth Owles, Roger Peers, Stephen Minnitt, Martin Broomfield, Dr John Prag, Georgina Plowright, Mary Cra'ster, Dr Andrew Sherratt, Barbara Green and George Boon. The sources of photographed material are mentioned in the captions, and these institutions also supplied the photographs except for plates 6, 8, 9 and the cover picture, which were taken by Dave Jeffries. I am also grateful to Christine Martin, who read the text and typed the manuscript.

2
The early bronze age, 2600-1400 BC

Background

Metalworking, the ability to smelt ores and to work the resulting metal into a vast range of shapes, marks an important step in man's technological development. The manufacture of objects of copper, bronze and gold arose, however, not from a disinterested curiosity in the properties of matter, but from needs which were an integral part of the society which produced them.

Copper appears occasionally as nuggets of pure or 'native' copper, but generally it occurs as a mineral ore which must be refined by fire. There are important copper ore deposits on the Middle Eastern plateaux, in Turkey, Spain, the Balkans and Cyprus. The continental sources of greatest importance in British prehistory are those of the north Alpine-Tyrolean area and of the Erzgebirge and Saxony in Germany, together perhaps with those of Brittany. In the British Isles deposits occur in Devon and Cornwall, North Wales, western Scotland and south-western Ireland.

Tin is rarer, but tin ore, cassiterite, occurs again in the Middle East, in Spain and, most importantly, in the north Alpine and German ore-bearing regions. The largest north Atlantic deposits are in south-western Britain, but there are small deposits in Scotland, Ireland and Brittany which may have been significant in the bronze age. Prehistoric bronze was generally an alloy of 10 per cent tin and 90 per cent copper, with sometimes the addition of various other metals, especially lead in Britain.

Gold occurs as pure metal in most of the metalliferous areas of Europe, although it is rare. The largest north Atlantic deposits are those in the Wicklow Mountains of east-central Ireland.

The pyrotechnology needed to work metal must have drawn upon neolithic techniques of heat control in potting, which had reached considerable distinction by the beginning of the bronze age. Metalworking, initially of copper and gold, could have been first invented in one specific centre, from which it spread to the rest of the old world. Those who take this view usually favour the Middle Eastern plateaux as the centre. Alternatively, copper-working could have developed spontaneously anywhere with raw materials, fire technology and a society which wanted precious objects. There is evidence that this did happen, independently, in the Middle East, in the Balkans and possibly in Spain. South-

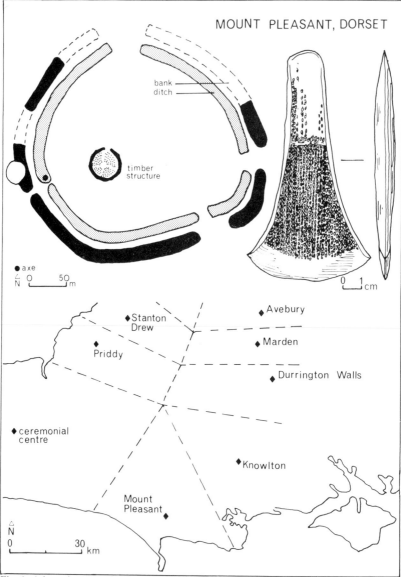

Fig. 1. A large henge and a decorated axe with slight flanges and bevel from a ditch at the west entrance of the henge, Mount Pleasant (Dorset) (after G. Wainwright). Around 2000 BC, and during the currency of axes like this, the central structure was replaced by a stone 'cove' and a timber palisade was erected inside the ditch. The map suggests territories based on ceremonial centres.

western Britain also possessed ores and a tradition of first-class potting, but nothing suggests independent development here. In British society metallurgy was an exotic craft, and throughout the bronze age the British smiths continued to receive important foreign inspiration.

Use of copper in southern Britain

The use of copper began in southern Britain around 2600 BC as one element in a society which was becoming extremely complex. Evidence from Fengate in East Anglia suggests that in some places extensive land allotment systems with properly laid-out enclosures were being developed, although many, perhaps most, communities still fed themselves from irregular corn plots and traditional areas of rough grazing. This society had well developed networks for the exchange of stone tools, and it manufactured elaborate pots like the Grooved Wares.

Most conspicuous are the great ceremonial henge complexes, like Avebury (Wiltshire) or Mount Pleasant (Dorset) (fig. 1). These are the central places of social territories where communities gathered at the right time of year. Their construction required considerable organised labour, and the impressive rites that took place at them must have been performed by priests: we can perceive the existence of an upper class, which desires prestigious metal goods and can gratify that desire through its control of exchange systems and craftsmen.

Similar élites appeared at the same time in Ireland and on the continent of Europe. Their emergence and their use of metal are closely linked with the crucial, but still enigmatic, appearance across this wide area of the phenomenon known as the *beaker tradition,* the origins of which have been sought chiefly in Iberia and the Rhineland. This included not only the fine beaker pots (e.g. fig. 2, plate 1) but also copper daggers, stone wristguards (if that is what they are), barbed and tanged arrowheads, V-perforated buttons and double-pointed awls. This artefact cluster is clearly recognisable wherever it occurs, as at Barnack (Cambridgeshire) (plate 1). However, it does not seem to have been accompanied by new forms of settlement or, essentially, of ritual monument, but rather to have enriched existing traditions. It has been variously interpreted as evidence for a series of folk migrations, for the rapid spread of a compelling religious cult, or for the swift dissemination of a new fashion which the best people everywhere had to have. These interpretations are not mutually exclusive, and they all point to a stratified society ripe for copper,

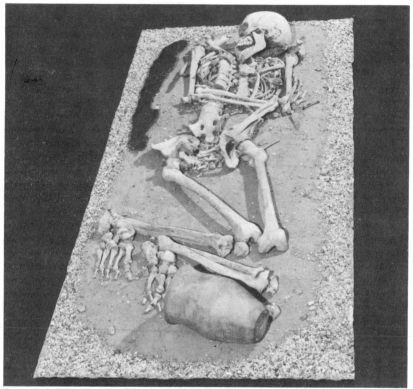

Plate 1. Grave group from Barnack (Cambridgeshire). An adult male inhumation was accompanied by a large beaker (height 240 mm, 9½ inches), a tanged dagger, a looped pendant of bone or walrus ivory (right, above) and a 'wristguard' of polished greenstone with its perforations capped with gold (right, below). The burial seems to have been in a wooden structure and lay at the base of a barrow (British Museum).

gold and (finally) bronze.

The earliest British metalwork seems to have been inspired by both central/north-western European and Irish traditions, the first deriving from 'international' or early Rhenish beaker traditions, and the second from Iberian beaker or proto-beaker innovations. The tanged copper dagger found in a burial at Roundway (Wiltshire) with its copper pin, its 'wristguard', arrowhead and beaker belong in the 'international' beaker style (fig. 2). The dagger from Mere (Wiltshire) is similar, but the gold disc found with it may be from Ireland, where such gold trinkets are much more common. The gold basket earrings, however, like those from Radley (Oxfordshire) (fig. 2), seem to be continental.

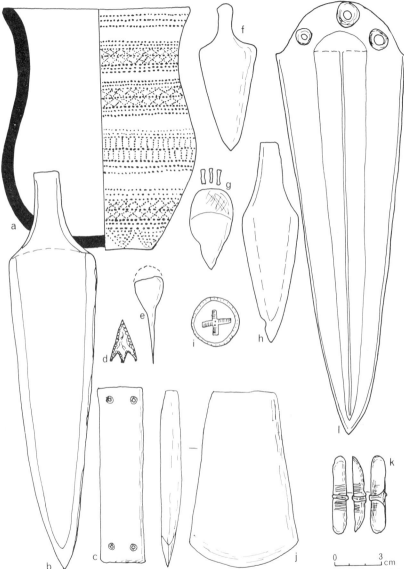

Fig. 2. a-e: Beaker, dagger, 'wristguard', arrowhead and pin; Roundway (Wiltshire) (after K. Annable and D. D. A. Simpson). **f, g:** Dagger, knife; Dorchester (Oxfordshire) (after C. Burgess). **h, i:** Dagger, gold disc; Mere (Wiltshire) (after Annable and Simpson). **j:** Flat axe; Slitter Cave, Cheddar (Somerset) (after S. Pearce). **k:** Gold earring; Radley (Oxfordshire) (*Inv. Arch.* GB 2). **l:** Halberd; Tonfannau Quarry (Gwynedd) (after W. Grimes).

The Dorchester grave (fig. 2) had, in addition to the dagger, a small knife with rivets to hold the handle: that this was an important technical advance is emphasised by the fact that one of the rivets was of bronze, already apparently sporadically in use.

The *Irish industry* concentrated on heavy flat axes, followed by large numbers of halberds. Some of these types in Britain, especially western Britain, are probably Irish imports, but others were made in British workshops. The axe sequence begins with straight-sided, thick, broad-butt copper implements (known as the Castletown Roche type from a find in Ireland) like that from Slitter Cave, Cheddar (fig. 2), followed by thick, broad-butt pieces with curving sides (Irish Lough Ravel). The next group (Irish Ballybeg) has curving sides and fairly broad, thin butts, a feature possibly developed in Britain. The axe hoard from Moel Arthur (Clwyd) fits into this general category (plate 2). Halberd manufacture began at this stage, a fashion principally Irish, but also adopted by Welsh smiths, who produced weapons like the pair from Tonfannau (fig. 2). The thin-butt axes and the halberds correlate broadly with the earlier riveted daggers.

Local copper ores in Ireland, Scotland, Wales and south-western Britain were exploited throughout this period and some metal, perhaps in the form of, or for, daggers came from Europe, but bulk quantities of Irish copper seem to have been the backbone of the British industries (Burgess 1980, Stages I to III).

The earliest bronzeworking

The earliest bronzeworking is often called the *Migdale-Marnoch* stage, from two important Scottish finds. Its products are better recognised in the north than elsewhere in Britain, but there is important material from the southern part of the country. The use of tin bronze shows contacts with the central European early Unětician industries, around 2300 BC.

The main bronze types are developments from the preceding copper forms. The flat axes had narrower, thinner butts than the copper types, like that from Harlyn (Cornwall) (fig. 3). Knives and daggers had high, rounded butt ends, and they were equipped with a number of slender 'peg' rivets. Double-pointed awls, like that from Butterwick (North Yorkshire) (fig. 3), remained in production. Halberds of Tonfannau type still circulated, and a new form, the Breagwy, with a shortish triangular blade and multiple slender rivets, appeared, but neither type proved to be very popular throughout southern Britain.

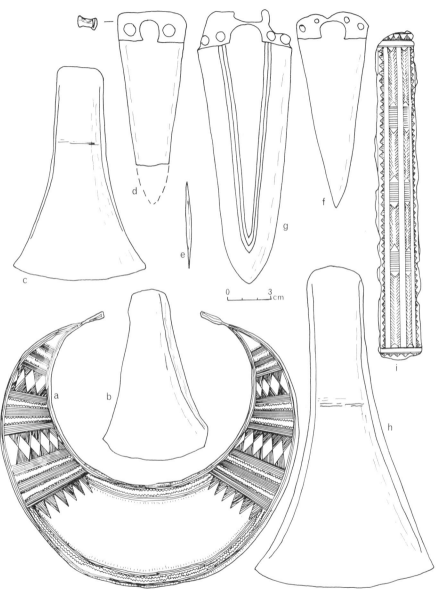

Fig. 3. a, b: Lunula, flat axe; Harlyn Bay (Cornwall) (after Pearce). **c, d:** Flat axe, dagger; Parwick (Derbyshire) (*Inv. Arch.* GB 19). **e:** Awl; Butterwick (North Yorkshire) (after Burgess). **f–h:** Two daggers, flat axe; Aylesford (Kent) (after Burgess). **i:** Armring; Knipton (Leicestershire) (*Inv. Arch.* GB 20).

Plate 2. Hoard of broad, thin-butt copper axes (length of longest 157 mm, 6¼ inches); Moel Arthur (Clwyd) (Manchester Museum).

The finds from the grave group at Aylesford (Kent) show how types developed (fig. 3). The axe has the beginnings of raised edges, or flanges, and a transverse bevel, showing that hafting now involved an angled haft and not just a straight stick with the end split. The decorated axe from Mount Pleasant is broadly contemporary (fig. 1), and so is that from a barrow at Parwick (Derbyshire) (fig. 3). The Aylesford daggers have fairly shallow butts, like that from Parwick, which also has the thick 'plug' rivets which became the standard for daggers of the next, Wessex I, phase.

The smiths and their customers had a considerable interest in ornaments, probably inspired by European fashions. Many of the sheet metal tubular beads, covers for conical buttons and armrings come from the north, but a typically incised piece was found with a burial at Knipton (Leicestershire) (fig. 3).

Basket-shaped earrings, probably of both bronze and gold, were still being worn — perhaps newly made, perhaps as heirlooms. By far the most conspicuous gold pieces are the great gold collars, or lunulae, made of fairly thick sheet metal decorated with incised patterns. Most of these come from Ireland, but there is a thin scatter across Highland Britain and in north-west France. Dating is difficult, but two were found at

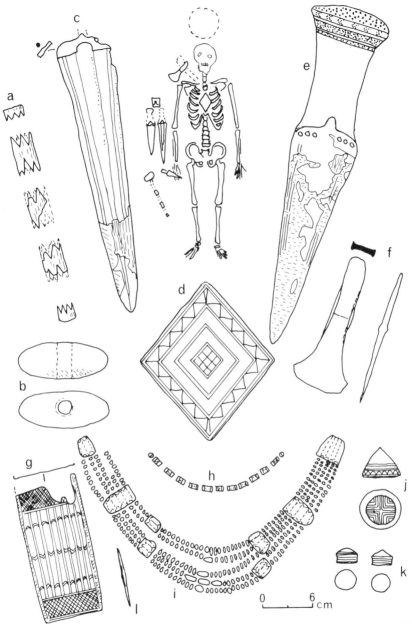

Fig. 4. a-f: Bone mounts, limestone mace head, dagger, gold plate, dagger with (reconstructed) pommel decorated with minute gold pins, flanged axe; Bush Barrow (Wiltshire) (after Annable and Simpson). The reconstruction shows also a gold belt hook, third dagger and possible shield above the head (after P. Ashbee). **g-l:** Gold plate, gold beads, amber necklace with complex-bored spacer beads, shale button with gold cover, two gold cones, awl; Upton Lovell (Wiltshire) (after Annable and Simpson).

Harlyn (fig. 3) probably with the flat axe, and it seems likely that lunulae were current throughout the Migdale phase, although some may have been made a little earlier. Probably most of the lunulae were made in Ireland, although provincial versions were produced in Britain. Lunulae are clearly ceremonial objects, but they are not found in graves, which suggests that they descended from person to person as insignia of rank or office, possibly hereditary. Their absence from central and eastern Britain hints that here social customs were different.

Some Irish copper continued to arrive and the exploitation of local British ores was increased, but in lowland Britain the use of continental metal expanded considerably (Stages IV to V).

The Wessex culture and contemporary metal

The period around 2000 BC, during the currency of bronzes like those from Aylesford, saw social changes, demonstrated by the sealing of many ancient chambered tombs, the end of henge building, new uses for the great ceremonial centres, and a new approach to burial rites in which cremation burial gradually ousted inhumation and vast numbers of barrows and ring monuments were built across the countryside. The burials demonstrate great social divisions. Much of the metalwork comes from the rich graves of the Wessex chalklands and, sporadically, from southern Britain generally: these graves seem to be the burials of chieftains, and their distribution suggests a series of territorial chiefdoms.

The first Wessex phase is called the *Wessex I* or Bush Barrow phase, after its most famous find (fig. 4). After prolonged discussion, the phase is now dated between about 1800 and 1600 BC. The Bush Barrow (Wiltshire) shows the range of types. The inhumed body was accompanied by prestigious sheet gold ornaments, by a small axe with hammered-up side flanges, better suited to the new angled hafts than the old, larger pieces, and by three daggers. Two daggers survive, both of the Armorico-British series, which appears on both sides of the English Channel; one is flat, of Armorico-British A type, and the other is of Armorico-British B type, with midrib. The former had a gold-mounted pommel. Similar gold ornaments, an awl and one of the elaborate amber necklaces which echo the lunulae came from the contemporary barrow from Upton Lovell (Wiltshire) (fig. 4), and from a barrow on the Dorset Ridgeway comes a group like that from Bush Barrow (fig. 5). The great gold cape from Mold (Clwyd) is

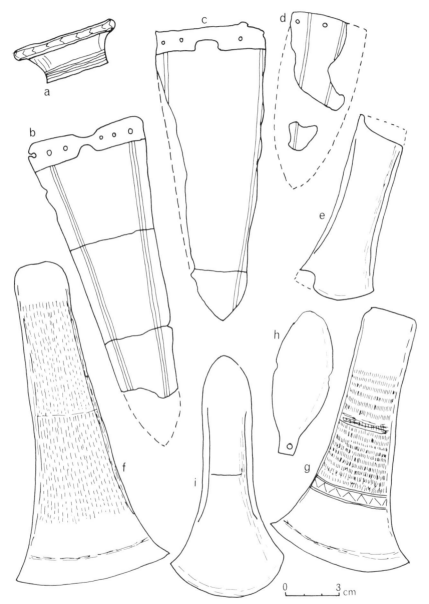

Fig. 5. a-e: Gold pommel, three daggers, flanged axe; Ridgeway (Dorset) (after Pearce).
f, g: Flat axes; Willerby Wold (North Yorkshire) (after Burgess). **h:** razor; Priddy
(Somerset). **i:** Flanged axe; Lannacombe (Devon) (both after Pearce).

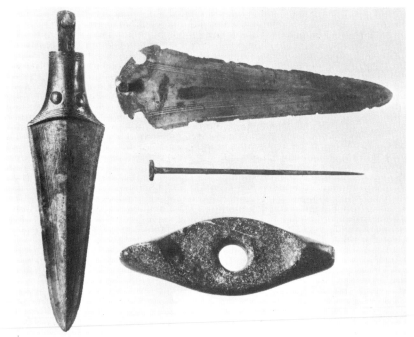

Plate 3. Grave group from Snowshill (Gloucestershire) with stone battleaxe, crutch-headed pin, Snowshill dagger and tanged-and-collared spearhead (length 240 mm, 9½ inches) (British Museum).

probably contemporary. The Class 1a razor (fig. 5) from a burial at Priddy on Mendip demonstrates the tools in the service of the chiefs.

Finds of axes, like the decorated examples from Willerby Wold (North Yorkshire) (fig. 5) or the hammered-flange axe from Lannacombe (Devon) (fig. 5) or the hoards of decorated axes from St Erth and Trenovissick (Cornwall) tend to appear beyond Wessex. They may be part of a western social tradition geared not to rich chieftains and their burials but still to the lunulae wearers.

As in the preceding phase, local ores continued to be exploited, while copper and probably gold came from Ireland, and bronze from Europe. This ties in with the close connection between the Bush Barrow chiefs and their counterparts in Armorica, confirmed by the daggers and the gold-nailed pommels, and it must be the background to the finds of British amber spacer beads in central Europe and the Mycenean Aegean (Stage VI).

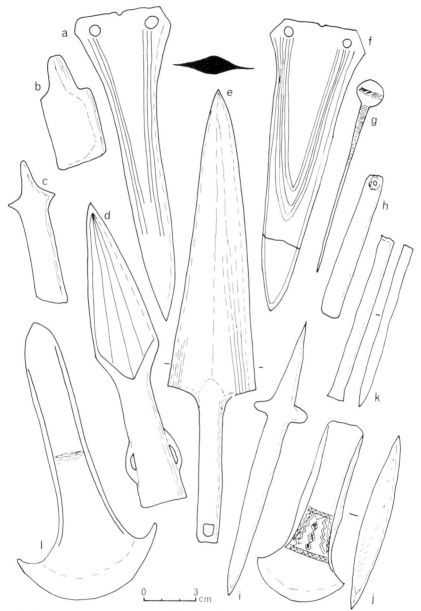

Fig. 6. a-d: Dagger, two punches, side-looped spearhead; Ebnal (Shropshire) (after C. Burgess and J. Cowen). **e:** Tanged spearhead; Burwell Fen (Cambridgeshire) (after S. Needham). **f-h:** Dagger, pin, whetstone; Camerton barrow (Avon). **i, j:** Punch, flanged axe; Westbury-on-Trym (Avon) (all Bristol City Museum). **k, l:** Punch, flanged axe; Plymstock (Devon) (*Inv. Arch.* GB 9).

The *Wessex II* phase, also called the Aldbourne-Edmonsham phase, spans the period from about 1600 to 1400 BC. Its characteristic Camerton and Snowshill daggers have ogival outlines, grooved blades and strong plug rivets, usually in threes. A range of decorative pins was fashionable (fig. 6, plate 3). Precious cups, like that in corrugated goldwork from a barrow at Rillaton (Cornwall), were highly regarded (plate 4) and are one link with a range of related material in the Swiss/south German area, to which southern Britain was now orientated by way of northern France.

The daggers in these graves, and other similar daggers, seem to have been the products of smiths working in the *Arreton* tradition, so-called from a famous find from the Isle of Wight (plate 5), and the equivalent to the Irish Inch Island workshops. Arreton smiths also produced the new cast flanged axes (fig. 6, plate 5) and two types of spearhead: those with a tang, often pierced for a rivet, and those with a cast hollow socket, a major design advance (fig. 6). The Snowshill spearhead is a hybrid of the two and represents the experimental stage (plate 3). The smiths also developed a range of lugged and shouldered chisels and the longer, slimmer Class 1b razors, which were to last a long time (plate 8).

Arreton material is distributed mostly in south-east Britain and along the south coast. The Welsh Marches produced their own version of the industry, represented by the find from *Ebnal* (Shropshire) (fig. 6). Ebnal products included socketed spearheads with solid cast heads and loops on the sockets, a link with the similar products of the Inch Island smiths (Stage VII).

The bulk of Arreton-Ebnal material comes not from barrows but as solitary pieces or as group finds. The groups are mixtures of axes, weapons and tools and probably represent the output of the workshops. In character, the finds look back to the axe groups of the past and forward to the groups of Acton Park/Taunton phase material rather than to the rich burials of their contemporaries. Their distribution outside Wessex, close to the Irish and continental metal sources, and also close, perhaps, to land like Dartmoor, ripe for more determined exploitation, suggests the rise of new social groups, which, by the end of the Arreton tradition, had eclipsed the barrow chiefs.

Plate 4. Sheet gold cup (height 70 mm, 2¾ inches) found with a Camerton dagger in a cist under a barrow; Rillaton (Cornwall) (British Museum).

Plate 5. Part of a find from Arreton (Isle of Wight) with two tanged spearheads, two cast-flanged axes, a dagger, a socketed spearhead (length 225 mm, 8⅞ inches) and a tanged spearhead (British Museum).

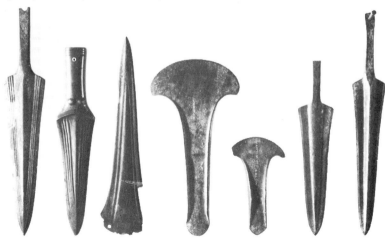

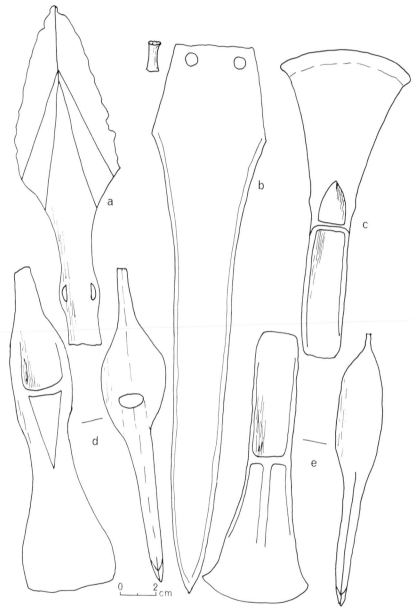

Fig. 7. a: Side-looped spear; Glastonbury (Somerset) (after Pearce). **b:** Dirk and rivet; Sion Reach (London) (after M. Rowlands). **c:** Shield pattern palstave; Chepstow Bridge (Gloucestershire) (after Burgess). **d:** Crediton palstave; Veryan (Cornwall) (after Pearce). **e:** Ribbed palstave; Chepstow (Gwent) (after Burgess).

3
The middle bronze age, 1400-1200 BC

Background

By around 1400 BC the social changes, which eventually created large areas of arable fields surrounding homesteads of the kind which can still be seen on Dartmoor (fig. 11), had begun to have a more obvious effect upon the character of the metal industries. The new metal types which the farming community required justify the division into a new industrial phase. The novel forms of axes, rapiers and spearheads began to be developed in the first phase of the middle bronze age, known as the *Acton Park* phase after an important find from Clwyd (Stage VIII). Their development, accompanied by ornaments and tools, continued in the following *Taunton* phase, which began soon after 1400 BC, and which is so called because an especially rich series of finds has been made in the Vale of Taunton (Stage IX).

The Acton Park industries

Palstaves are the backbone of the middle bronze age industries. They are a technical improvement on the earlier flanged axe for the flanges and the stop of a palstave are run together and heightened to form a firmer seating for the split, knee-shaft handle. They must have worked, because they continued in use for so long, but they strike modern workers as an extremely inept and clumsy design. Many archaeologists have laboured long over the division of palstaves into types and into relative chronologies but many finer points are unresolved and are likely to remain so.

Nonetheless, we can form a good idea of their general history. The earliest palstaves were large, rugged pieces with fairly wide blades, and often with an uncouth, tentative appearance. They lack side loops but were often cast with knobs on the outside of the flanges; these helped to secure the thong binding the axehead to the handle. These early palstaves often had their blades decorated with a midrib (Group 1 type) like that from Chepstow (fig. 7), or with a shield pattern (Group 2 type).

Early midrib and shield pattern palstaves were being manufactured by the Acton Park smiths of North Wales and by smiths in eastern Britain before 1400 BC. The Crediton-type palstaves of south-western Britain may well begin as early (fig. 7). Beside the palstaves, the smiths were producing a range of improved flanged axes, which culminated in the haft-flanged types with higher flanges and a bar stop, and these were the normal axe form in northern Britain. It is still not clear whether the palstave was a British invention, developed either in North Wales or in eastern Britain, or whether it was inspired by North German forms.

The new dirks and rapiers were inspired by lozenge-hilted weapons which appeared over much of Europe. The two weapon types are very similar, but the conventional division is at 355 mm (14 inches); a piece shorter than this is termed a dirk, and one longer a rapier. Rapiers and dirks were stabbing weapons with slender straight-sided blades and flat trapeze-shaped hilts to which handles were riveted with, in the early stages, two rivets.

Rapiers are usually divided on the basis of their blade cross-sections. Early, or Group I, weapons have a midrib which betrays their ancestry in earlier bronze age dagger forms. Group II weapons have lozenge-section blades, sometimes further refined by the addition of bevelled blade edges (fig. 7). Midrib and then lozenge-bladed forms were manufactured by Acton Park smiths and their eastern and south-western contemporaries. The same smiths were producing fully socketed spearheads, with side loops on the sockets. The loops were intended to carry the thong helping to fasten the spearhead to the shaft. These spearheads have leaf-shaped blades or, sometimes, kite-shaped blades, which may be an Irish trait (fig. 7). Smiths and their customers had available Class 1b razors, simple chisels, both with and without side lugs, and single-pointed awls, but the range of tools was very restricted, and there was, surprisingly, no interest in the production of metal ornaments.

The Taunton industries: axes and weapons

The palstave industries developed steadily from their Acton Park origins, with the pieces retaining their wide blades, but becoming overall rather lighter and more elegant as the period progressed. Side loops became a regular feature. Palstaves with ribbed decoration, like those from Cemmaes (Powys) (fig. 8), remained popular, and so did shield decorated forms. Some designs seem to have particular regional distributions. 'Werrar' palstaves, for example, (fig. 8) are centred upon the Isle of Wight. The palstaves mentioned so far belong in the 'low-flanged' group, with shallow side flanges, but in south-western Britain high side-flanged pieces like that from Edington Burtle (fig. 8) were popular, known as the 'south-western' type. Flanged axes were still the dominant type in the north, but the occasional wing-flanged piece does occur in southern Britain, like that from

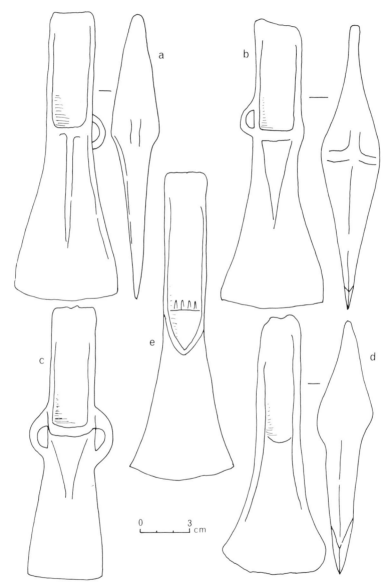

Fig. 8. a: Ribbed palstave; Cemmaes (Powys) (after Grimes). **b:** South-western palstave; Edington Burtle (Somerset) (*Inv. Arch.* GB 44). **c:** Double-looped palstave; Curland (Somerset). **d:** Winged-flanged axe; Tredarvah (Cornwall) (both after Pearce). **e:** Werrar palstave; Arreton (Isle of Wight) (after Rowlands).

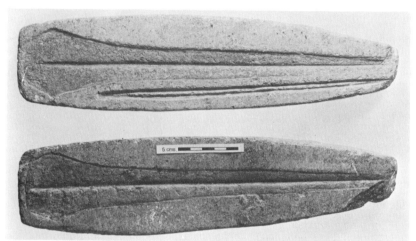

Plate 6: Bivalve stone mould for lozenge-section dirk; Holsworthy (Devon). One valve also has a matrix for a ribbed strip (Holsworthy Museum).

Tredarvah (fig. 8), which probably belongs at the very end of the phase.

Lozenge-section rapiers continued to be made and used, and this is one factor which makes the relative dating of finds difficult. The stone dirk mould found at Holsworthy in Devon (plate 6), comprising two valves which fit together with a vent at the top through which the metal would be poured, would produce lozenge-section pieces. No precise date can be given for their use within the Acton Park-Taunton range. Nevertheless, rapier technology did improve, with the production of the splendid Group III triple-arris (or triple-ridged) rapiers, like that from Badbury Rings (Dorset) (fig. 9), which are a peak of the bronzesmiths' art. Towards the end of the Taunton phase production of the Group IV flat-rib rapiers commenced, but many of these seem to belong more happily with the Penard traditions (see below).

Leaf-shaped, side-looped spearheads were produced through-out the period (fig. 9). They were used for fighting (plate 7). In the mature Taunton phase they were joined by leaf-shaped, basal-looped spearheads (fig. 9), which were perhaps an aerodynamic improvement.

The Taunton industries: tools and ornaments

Early razors, lugged chisels and bar chisels remained available to the Taunton smiths and their customers, but they were joined

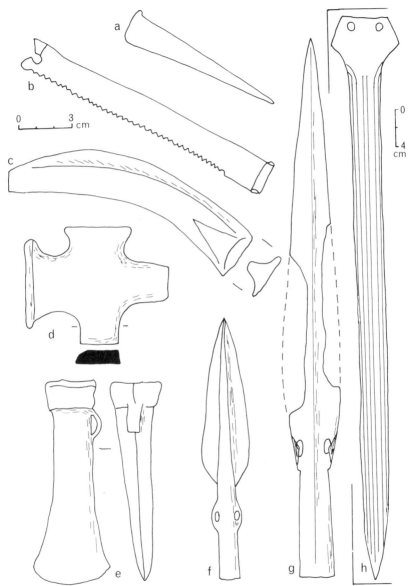

Fig. 9. a, b: Chisel, saw blade; Monkton (Dyfed) (after Grimes). **c:** Sickle blade; Edington Burtle (Somerset) (*Inv. Arch.* GB 44). **d:** Anvil; Bishopsland (County Kildare) (after G. Eogan). **e:** Socketed tool; Axbridge (Somerset) (after Pearce). **f:** Side-looped spearhead; Datchet (Berkshire) (after Rowlands). **g:** Basal-looped spearhead; Sherford (Somerset) (*Inv. Arch.* GB 45). **h:** Triple-arris rapier; Badbury (Dorset) (after Pearce).

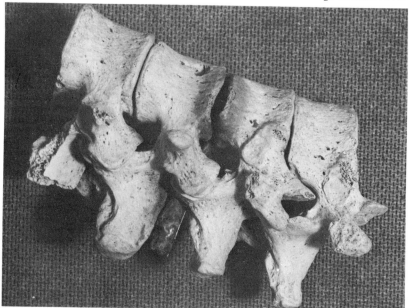

Plate 7. The broken-off blade of a side-looped spearhead embedded in human lumbar vertebrae; Tormarton (Avon) (Bristol City Museum).

by new forms like the knobbed sickle blades from the Somerset finds (fig. 9), saw blades like that from Monkton (fig. 9), socketed hammers and socketed tools, probably used by woodworkers, often known as Taunton-Hademarschen types after two important finds from Taunton (plate 8) and from north Germany. Small bronze anvils, very like the larger iron forms in use to this day, were developed to assist the metalworkers. These are not common, and the best preserved is that in the contemporary find from Bishopsland (County Kildare) (fig. 9).

Detailed study of the south-western material, such as the large, varied and very important find from the Taunton Workhouse site (plate 8), suggests that these new tools begin in the mature phase of the Taunton industries, but they are also important in the succeeding Penard phase, and the line between the two phases is sometimes hard to draw.

Ornaments are so eyecatching a feature of the Taunton finds that the phase has often been called 'The Ornament Horizon'. The ornaments include the big, magnificently executed, spiral twisted neckrings or torcs and similar but smaller armrings, a range of annular and penannular armrings made of bar bronze, sometimes incised with decorative panels, ribbed armrings and

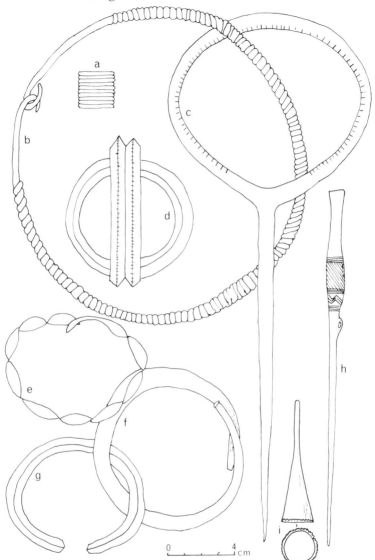

Fig. 10. a: Ribbed finger ring; Lakenheath (Suffolk) (after Rowlands). **b:** Twisted neckring; Barton Bendish (Norfolk) (*Inv. Arch.* GB 7). **c:** Quoit-headed pin, East Dean (West Sussex). **d:** Sussex loop; Hollingbury (East Sussex) (both after Rowlands). **e:** Ribbon bracelet; Edington Burtle (Somerset) (*Inv. Arch.* GB 44). **f:** Armring; Haselbury Bryan (Dorset). **g:** Armring; Evershot (Dorset) (both after Pearce). **h:** Side-looped pin; river Thames (after Rowlands). **i:** Cone; Monkswood (Gloucestershire) (*Inv. Arch.* GB 42).

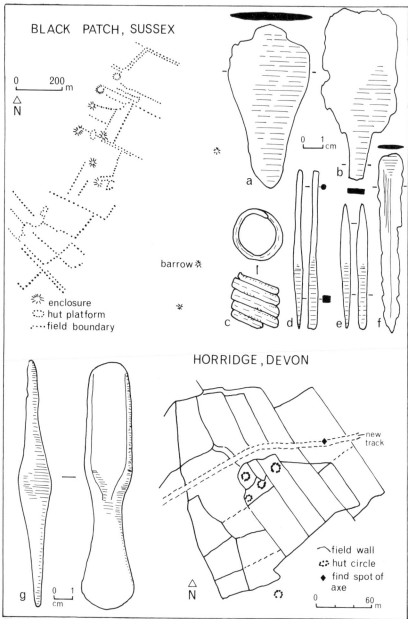

Fig. 11. Field system and bronzes from huts; Black Patch (Sussex). **a-f:** Tanged blade, early (Class 1) razor, coiled finger ring, two awls or tracers, knife (after P. Drewett). Field system and, **g,** Bohemian axe; Horridge, Dartmoor (Devon) (after A. Fox and D. Britton).

Plate 8. Part of a hoard from the Workhouse site, Taunton (Somerset). *Top:* Two Crediton palstaves from the same mould (length 167 mm, 6½ inches), twisted torc, Class 1b razor, ring. *Bottom:* Part of a sickle blade, developed shield pattern palstave, socketed 'Taunton' tool, socketed hammer, quoit-headed pin (Somerset County Museum).

finger rings, coiled finger rings and pins, some with side loops and some with large 'quoit' heads. There are also the curiously formed 'Sussex loops', presumed to be armrings, a range of lighter armrings, such as those decorated with repoussé work from Norton Fitzwarren or that twisted from a 'ribbon' of bronze from Edington Burtle, and oddities like the cones from Monkswood, which may be early spear ferrules (figs. 10, 12; plates 8-9).

These ornaments cluster most thickly in Somerset and Dorset and in East Anglia. They are represented in Cornwall, along the south coast and in the lower Thames valley, but beyond these areas their range and quantity rapidly decreases. Again, study of the south-western finds suggests that the heavy pieces, the torcs and the solid armrings, begin at the beginning of the phase and carry on through, but that the lighter armrings, the quoit-headed pins and the rococo Sussex loops were also developments of the mature Taunton industries.

All the ornaments mentioned so far are of bronze. In Ireland the equivalent pieces were sometimes of gold, and gold forms are occasionally found in southern Britain. However, these gold pieces appear to belong at the very end of the Taunton phase, and they have more in common with the immediately following Penard industries.

Foreign contacts

The social changes which took place in Britain also happened generally across central Europe, where their new expression is called the Tumulus Culture, and in north-western France and the Low Countries. The Acton Park phase in Britain and the Tréboul phase in Brittany saw the beginning of a detailed correspondence between the bronze forms produced in the two areas; with local differences of emphasis from time to time, this was to last until the end of the bronze age and can be explained only by incessant cross-Channel traffic that carried smiths, metal goods and, no doubt, other men and materials as well. The Voorhout find, made in Holland, bears this out very well. It contained North Welsh shield pattern palstaves, made of North Welsh metal, and also a lugged chisel of the type that remained in use for a very long time.

This parallelism continued in the Taunton period, although here links with the industries of Normandy and Picardy, and so eastwards into central France, were of special significance. The great find from Malassis had an extensive range of familiar Taunton types, including palstaves, rapiers, basal-looped spearheads, knobbed sickles, armrings and spiral rings. It looks as if the novel forms of the Ornament Horizon were manufactured in northern France on the basis of ideas produced by the Nordic and Tumulus smiths further east and were transmitted to British metalworkers, who extended the range. The new tools of the Taunton phase, however, especially socketed chisel-like pieces and the socketed hammers, may have been invented in the Taunton area, and from there the former passed to northern Europe, where a number of examples have been found.

Metal analysis of the bronze finds shows that local metal sources, including the south-western tin, were exploited during the period, but, surprisingly, apparently only for relatively local use. The smiths of south-eastern and south-central Britain mostly used metal coming initially from northern France, and ultimately from the great ore-refining centres of central and Alpine Europe. It seems to have arrived as bronze, probably made up into French

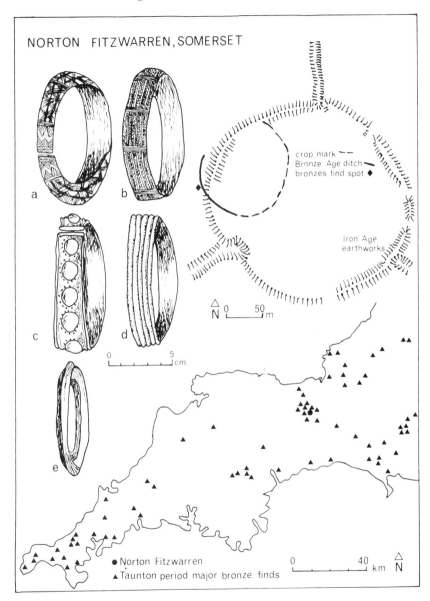

Fig. 12. Enclosure and, **a-e,** two incised armrings, repoussé decorated armring, ribbed armring, lozenge-section armring; Norton Fitzwarren (Somerset) (after N. Langmaid).

palstaves, like some in the find from Pear Tree Green (Hampshire), and was reworked in Britain. The central European palstave from Horridge (Devon) (fig. 11) is a precious piece of direct evidence for the longer link. The evidence for the flow of the metal and the similarities in the designs being produced in southern Britain and France together make good sense.

Metalwork in Taunton society

Acton Park and Taunton phase metal is sometimes found in groups, multiple finds often called 'hoards'. This term is probably misleading in that it lumps together two different kinds of find. The south-western evidence, at least, suggests that one type of multiple find typically includes a relatively large range of axes, large and small ornaments, tools and the odd weapon, often in used condition or even fragmented, scattered over a limited area and mixed with household debris like pots, bones and charcoal. Where the evidence is sufficient, it is clear that such finds often come from settlement sites. The Taunton Workhouse find has a characteristic range, and so does the material from Black Patch (Sussex) (fig. 11).

The other find type comprises a smaller number of pieces, usually large ornaments like neckrings and heavy armrings or axes, or sometimes both, in very good condition, not mixed with rubbish and apparently often carefully concealed together in what was a conspicuous field monument at the time of the burial. The term 'hoard' is better reserved for finds like these. The Egglesham, Dorchester, hoard is a good example (plate 9), and so are the two axes from Veryan (Cornwall) (fig. 7) found buried in a bronze age field bank, or the hoard from Mulfra (Cornwall) found concealed in the mound of Mulfra Quoit, a chambered tomb already of great antiquity at that time. The armrings and axes from Norton Fitzwarren (fig. 12), originally probably tied together, are another true hoard.

It looks as if the scattered finds are just the remains of bronze in daily use, while the hoards seem to be accumulations of wealth. They could be negotiable capital, acquired by an individual through the network of deals and detailed negotiations which characterise small-scale societies, and expended for a specific social purpose, like satisfaction for a killing or the purchase of a bride. They could be deposits offered to the gods.

Scatters like the Taunton Workhouse find, which had tools and fragments due to be melted down, seem to be the remains of bronzeworking shops. The general character of these finds

Plate 9. Hoard of two annular armrings (diameter about 85 mm, 3⅜ inches) and two palstaves, south-west and developed shield pattern; Egglesham Meadow, Dorchester (Dorset) (Dorset County Museum).

suggests that the smith was a small-scale craftsman, perhaps even part-time, who worked in direct association with a customer, who perhaps ordered only one piece at a time. There are suggestions of a superior class in Taunton Britain — the men who wore the rapiers and who conducted the cross-Channel metal trade — but these do not emerge visibly as entrepreneurs who controlled both metal supply and smiths. In spite of all the difficult problems associated with artefact distribution, the bronze finds in south-west Britain do seem to show several well marked clusters, like that in the Vale of Taunton, which includes Norton Fitzwarren (fig. 12). These hint at firmly established farming communities in whose hands bronze wealth was concentrated.

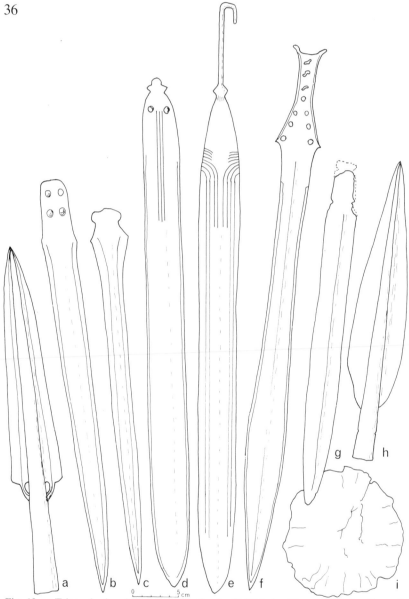

Fig. 13. a: Triangular basal-looped spear; Combe St Nicholas (Somerset) (after Pearce).
b: Lambeth sword; river Thames (after V. Megaw and D. D. A. Simpson). **c-d:** Flat-rib
rapier, Monza sword; Eriswell (Suffolk) (after B. Trump). **e:** Rixheim sword; off
Salcombe (Devon) (after K. Muckleroy and P. Baker). **f:** Hemigkofen sword; river
Thames (after Megaw and Simpson). **g-i:** Ballintober sword, late pegged spear, bronze
plate; Worth (Devon) (after Pearce).

4
The Penard and Wilburton industries, 1200-900 BC

Background

Around 1200 BC a climatic change to colder, wetter weather, the possible exhaustion of arable land and a probable growth in population resulted in social changes across northern Europe. In southern Britain, fields and settlements on Dartmoor and in the Fens were abandoned as the peat developed, causing the dislocation of Taunton phase patterns. Land was apparently divided afresh, and in some areas cattle herding became the chief means of livelihood. New forms of metalwork were part of the response to the new pressures. In southern and central Europe this is called the Early Urnfield period, and in southern Britain it is divided into two phases: the *Penard*, lasting from soon after 1200 to 1000 BC, and the *Wilburton*, from about 1000 to 900 BC.

In southern Britain during this whole period weaponry is very conspicuous. Some buried weapon hoards look like offerings to the gods of war, while others are probably personal arms. Gold ornaments and prestige objects made of sheet bronze, a new technique, appear, and so, in the Wilburton phase, do horse and wagon fittings. Axes and tools, on the other hand, are much less obvious than during the Taunton phase. As the period progressed, hilltop settlements began to be important, and these are probably 'high' politically and socially, as well as physically. All this suggests the emergence of a powerful, competitive warrior élite who controlled land, herds and peasant farmers, and also the output of the smiths and the distribution of metal.

Penard phase metalwork

During the Penard phase the continental sword tradition impinged upon the native rapier tradition, and by the end of the phase it had superseded it. Early Rixheim swords, typical of the Urnfield groups of central-west Europe, and characterised by straight-sided blades and rat's tail rod tangs, inspired the Monza sword series typical of Switzerland and north Italy and the Rosnoën swords of north-west France, with their flat hilt plates carrying four paired rivet holes; Rosnoën swords seem to lie behind the small group of very similar Lambeth swords found in southern Britain (fig. 13).

Meanwhile, in central Europe, the Erbenheim and Hemig-

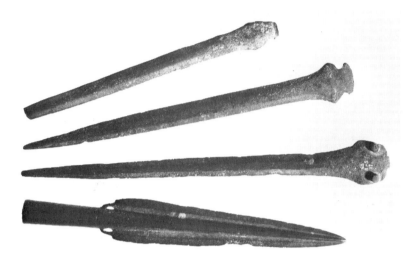

Plate 10: Hoard of three flat-rib rapiers and a triangular basal-looped spear (length 350 mm, 13¾ inches); Maentwrog (Gwynedd) (British Museum).

kofen swords had appeared, with leaf-shaped blades, flanged hilts with rivet holes to carry hilt plates, wide shoulders also with rivet holes, and sometimes ricassi, the blade notch below the shoulder, probably intended as a thumb grip. Smiths in southern Britain seem to have combined the Rosnoën/Lambeth and Hemigkofen swords to produce first the Chelsea type and then the Ballintober weapons, true swords with leaf-shaped blades and fairly wide shoulders, but with a flat, not flanged, hilt plate. There may also have been an element of fusion between rapiers and swords. This certainly produced the rare leaf-bladed rapiers with their thick, strong, flat midribs. The important find from Eriswell (Suffolk) with its Monza sword and standard flat-rib rapier makes a number of important points (fig. 13).

The side-looped and smaller leaf-shaped basal-looped spear-heads faded away, to be replaced by triangular basal-looped spearheads and by peg-hole spearheads, which had been entirely lacking in the Taunton repertoire. The important weapon finds from Worth (Devon) (fig. 13), which contained an early attempt at sheet metalworking with its two spearheads and Ballintober sword, and from Maentwrog (Gwynedd), with its flat-rib rapiers and triangular spearhead (plate 10), show the types and bring blades and spears together to show the new, heavily armed warrior.

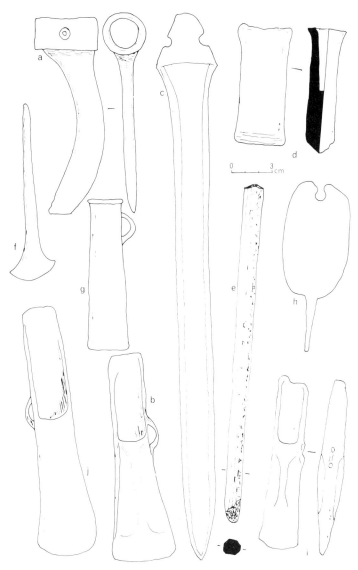

Fig. 14. a-c: Ring-socket sickle, narrow-bladed palstave, flat-rib rapier; Downham Market (Norfolk) (after Megaw and Simpson). **d-f:** Socketed hammer, metal bar, tanged chisel; Burgess Meadow, Oxford (*Inv. Arch.* GB 6). **g:** Socketed tool; Penard (Glamorgan). **h:** Bifid or Class 2 razor; river Thames (both after Megaw and Simpson). **i:** Narrow-bladed palstave; off Salcombe (Devon) (after Muckleroy and Baker). **j:** Narrow-bladed palstave; off Dover (Kent) (after S. Stevens).

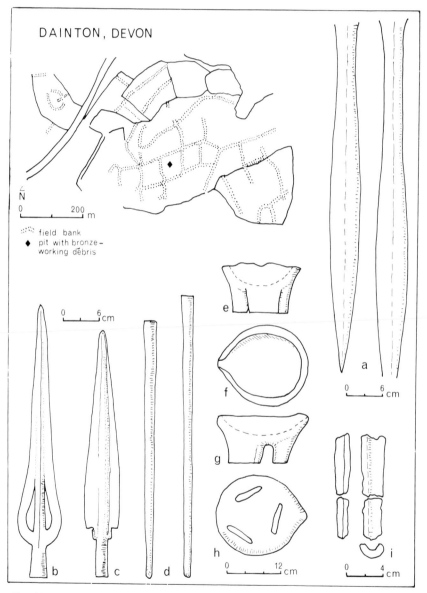

Fig. 15. a: Sword blades. **b:** Lunate-opening spearhead. **c:** Basal-looped spearhead. **d:** Ferrules, all reconstructed from mould fragments. **e-h:** Reconstruction of crucible viewed from front, above, side and below. **i:** Clay mould fragments from casting a ferrule. All from Dainton (Devon) (after Needham).

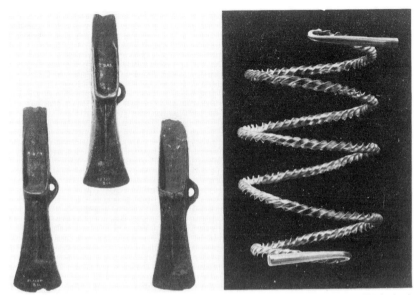

Plate 11. Group of three narrow-bladed palstaves (length of longest 190 mm, 7½ inches) and a gold composite twisted ornament; Grunty Fen (Cambridgeshire) (University Museum of Archaeology and Anthropology, Cambridge).

The great range of palstave types ceased to be manufactured although some continued to be used. In their place appeared narrow-bladed palstaves, but the small numbers which have been found suggest that axe hoards were no longer accumulated and that metal was carefully husbanded, to be repeatedly recast. Penard tools included ring-socket sickles, socketed hammers and chisels, tanged chisels and bifid, or Class 2, razors (fig. 14).

The elaborate gold ornaments, like those from Towednack (Cornwall) or Yeovil (Somerset) (illustrated on the front cover), which were made by twisting a composite bar of gold strips, technically an exceedingly difficult process, seem, from the few finds associated with bronzes like that from Grunty Fen (Cambridgeshire), found with narrow-bladed palstaves (plate 11), to begin in the Penard period, or possibly a little before. Such pieces could well have continued to be manufactured and certainly to be used for a considerable period. As a group they have strong Irish connections.

Penard-style metal is relatively rare, and much of it is concentrated in the lower Thames valley, although important material comes from further afield. Penard smiths probably used clay moulds, but we have little idea where their work was carried out. New conditions were matched by a major shift in the metal supply. A single alloy type dominates contemporary bronzework in south Britain and north France, although its European source is as yet unidentified. Bronze came to Britain from northern France as cargoes of scrap, like those found off Dover and off Salcombe (Devon) (fig. 14), but continual remelting of an apparently scarce commodity helped to create a pool of uniformly constituted but increasingly tired metal (Stage X).

Wilburton phase industries

A heavy emphasis on weaponry and on technically demanding casting are characteristic of the Wilburton industries throughout their run, but within the sequence it is possible to perceive an earlier group, represented by the finds from Dainton (Devon) (fig. 15), Nettleham (Lincolnshire) and Andover (Hampshire), and a later group represented by finds like those from Wilburton itself, Isleham (Cambridgeshire) and Guilsfield (Powys).

From the beginning, spearhead forms became more varied and more elaborate. The reconstructed clay mould fragments at Dainton would have produced a triangular, basal-looped spear (a Penard survival perhaps typical of upland areas) and a lunate-opening spear, a new type. With these went long tubular ferrules, difficult to cast, and intended both to give the spear more power and to look splendid. Also in the same group were leaf-shaped swords. The Andover group was a collection of waste metal, and its fragments included spearheads and ferrules, new hollow-bladed spearheads, another smithing feat, and broken chapes, similar to that from Guilsfield (fig. 16) but smaller. These fitted on to the end of a scabbard to protect it from wear from the sword tip and added to the impressive, flashing appearance the warrior presented. Various rings for fastening baldrics also formed part of the panoply.

Sword fragments from Andover, and probably the blade evidence from Dainton, show that these were examples of types with heavy leaf-shaped blades, slotted flanged hilts, either straight (V-shaped) or drooping (U-shaped) shoulders and rounded ricassi (fig. 16). Such flange-hilted swords are part of Wilburton traditions, although their manufacture may have begun by the end of the Penard period. The finest of these swords, judging by epic literature generally, will have had names and histories of their own.

Wilburton developments are known to us chiefly through three large finds of founders' scrap from Wilburton, Guilsfield and

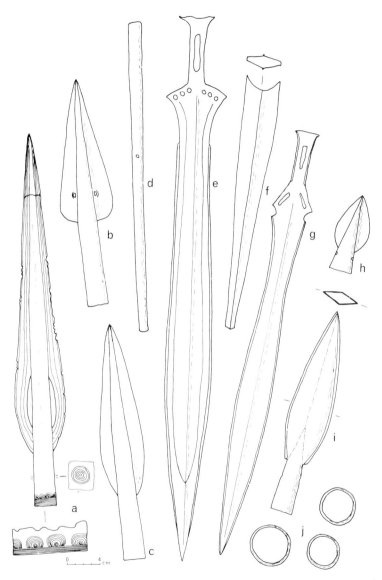

Fig. 16. a, h, j: Stepped-blade lunate-opening spearhead, short late pegged spear, rings, Blackmoor (Hampshire) (after I. Colquhoun). **b:** Protected opening spearhead; Ripon (North Yorkshire) (after Burgess). **c:** Late pegged spear: Burton upon Stather (Humberside) (*Inv. Arch.* GB 23). **d, f, i:** Long ferrule, long tongue chape, late pegged spearhead; Guilsfield (Powys) (after Grimes). **e:** U-butted sword; river Thames. **g:** V-butted sword; river Thames (both after Megaw and Simpson).

Plate 12. Part of a find from Isleham (Cambridgeshire). *Above:* Late Wilburton sword (length 600 mm, 23⅝ inches), tongue-shaped chape. *Left:* Pegged spear, tanged knife, cauldron ring, various fittings. *Centre:* Scrap, round phalera (broken). *Right:* Socketed axe, late palstave, various fittings (Moyses Hall Museum, Bury St Edmunds).

Isleham (plate 12), the last of which was enormous and contained a wide range of material probably accumulated over some time. The spearhead types and weapon accessories generally continue, although ferrules and chapes achieve exaggerated sizes. Sword types also continued, although Isleham included later types (see below), perhaps the latest pieces added to the group.

An important new element is the 'horsy' material, represented by horse bits from Wilburton and a range of harness pieces, like the 'phalerae' and other strap holders from Isleham. Isleham also had a variety of fittings for horse-drawn vehicles — wagons, or even chariots.

Wilburton weapons and related fittings were cast in clay moulds like those found at Dainton (fig. 15), some of which must have been very complex. Smiths began to add lead to bronze intended for accoutrements and complicated spears (although not for swords or simple spears) because this lowers molten metal temperatures and encourages flow, facilitating difficult castings where hardness is not important. The lead may have come from the Shropshire/northern Powys area, close to the Guilsfield find.

The fragments of a cauldron and a 'flesh hook' (for lifting out boiling joints) from Isleham show that sheet metalworking was well under way, and although many cauldrons and buckets come from undatable or late contexts sheet metal vessels were certainly being manufactured at this time. The technique of fastening sheet plates together with decorative rivets and adding heavy cast ring handles seems to have been a northern European not a Mediterranean idea. The circular bronze shields, whose beaten sheet metalwork represents a *tour de force* of the smiths' art, generally come from watery contexts and appear to be offerings. Dating is complicated, because they have not been found with anything else, but their manufacture, too, seems to have been a feature of Penard/Wilburton times (plate 13).

Tools were also produced (fig. 17). The large finds have a range of gouges, socketed axes, among which those with indented sides are very characteristic, and narrow-bladed late palstaves. Isleham also had a range of knives, possibly leatherworking tools, sickles and metalworkers' hammers. Nevertheless, tools are much less plentiful in the record than might be expected. The

Plate 13. Bronze shield of Yetholm type (diameter 648 mm, 25½ inches); Moel Siabod (Gwynedd) (British Museum).

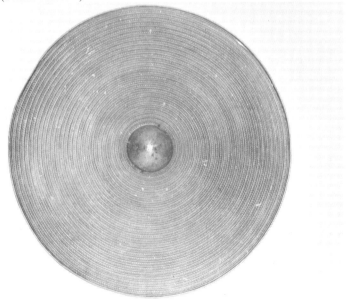

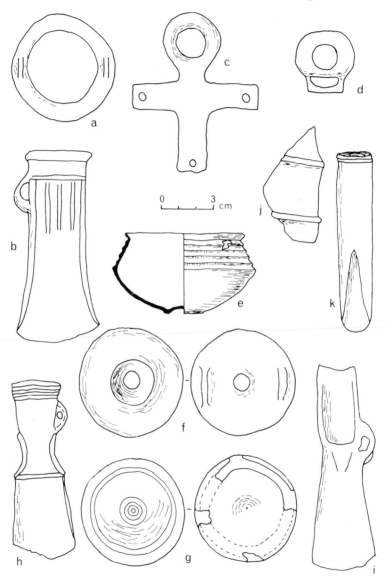

Fig. 17. a: Looped ring, Wilburton (Cambridgeshire) (University Museum, Cambridge). **b-g:** Socketed axe, handle attachment from bowl, ring with loop, bowl, disc mount with loops, disc slide; Welby (Leicestershire) (*Inv. Arch.* GB 24). **h-j:** Socketed axe, palstave, plate scrap metal; Isleham (Cambridgeshire) (Bury St Edmunds Museum). **k:** Socketed gouge; Guilsfield (Powys) (after Grimes).

repeated reuse of bronze and the dispersal of such pieces away from the great founders' accumulations may be among the reasons. Unlike the weaponry, tools seem to have been cast in bronze or stone moulds and to be made of bronze to which lead had not been deliberately added (although it was often present because it came to pervade the metal pool). Permanent moulds and a relatively simple technology would make for a more conservative and 'down-market' approach to tool production. There may well have been a social contrast between toolmakers and their customers on the one hand and weapon smiths and their lords on the other.

Wilburton industries relate closely to those of the St Brieuc-des-Iffs phase in northern France. In Britain, Wilburton types are now recognised as occurring throughout the south, although with concentrations in the Fens and the Thames valley. These clusters probably relate to the management of the metal supply, since Wilburton smiths used a very distinctive bronze alloy which came from Alpine or central Europe. This metal is linked with the new types and the new techniques, and presumably to the aristocratic class who wanted them.

There are signs in the finds from Guilsfield, Isleham and Sion Reach (London), all probably finally abandoned as Wilburton output came to an end, that this metal source was drying up. These finds, especially Isleham, have quantities of very unusual flat, ribbed plate scrap bronze (fig. 17), specially made from metal coming from a new source, although whether this was continental or British, and if so perhaps south-western British, is not yet clear. The plate scrap was a short-lived phenomenon, although the new sources it utilised remained important. The Wilburton tradition evolved very rapidly, and it faded just as fast, together with its characteristic organisation of metal supplies. Behind this history must lie specific, but now unknowable, political events.

Developments around 900 BC

There is a small number of finds with both later Wilburton material and types belonging in the subsequent Ewart Park phase. These transitional finds are very important in tracing the early development of the British Ewart Park industries, and especially of the native Ewart Park swords, although the problems posed are not yet fully resolved.

As already mentioned, the Isleham find included late Wilburton swords, with ricassi on their way to becoming straight (rather

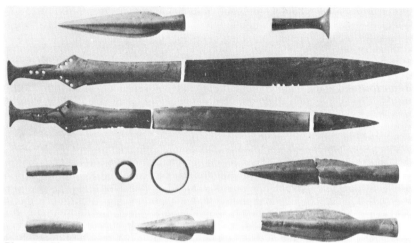

Plate 14. Find of two swords (length of longest 675 mm, 26½ inches), four pegged spearheads, a disc ferrule, rings and two hones; Marston St Lawrence (Northamptonshire) (British Museum).

than curved), a distinctive feature of Ewart Park swords. The find of weapon scrap from Blackmoor, Selborne (Hampshire), has a stress on spearheads, including stepped-bladed and lunate types, long tongue chapes, tubular ferrules and Wilburton sword fragments, all Wilburton types; but it also has small pegged spearheads of broad late Wilburton/Ewart Park range (fig. 16), a disc ferrule of transitional type, swords with straight ricassi and one sword fragment of 'proto Carp's Tongue' design (see below), all representing the beginnings of Ewart Park and contemporary industries. The weapon find from Marston St Lawrence (Northamptonshire), with a pair of Ewart Park swords, is very similar (plate 14).

The Welby find (Leicestershire) has bronze vessel fragments and horsy strap attachments, which link it with Isleham (fig. 17), but also a battered Ewart Park sword. The ribbed cast bowl is unique in southern Britain but would fit in the broad metal vessel context. The socketed axes in the Welby find link it with a number of post-Wilburton eastern finds with axes, like that from Burton upon Stather (Humberside) with some fourteen socketed axes, spears and bucket base plates (figs. 16, 19).

The Marston St Lawrence and Blackmoor finds contained significant quantities of Wilburton bronze alloy but also used alloys like those in the plate scrap, suggesting that in their access to metal supplies as in their types they are transitional.

5
The late bronze age, 900-600 BC

The Ewart Park phase

The axe hoards which appeared to the north and south of the Thames in the post-Wilburton phase heralded the immense development of bronze industries which characterised the earlier late bronze age from about 900 BC to about 700 BC. The period as a whole is usually called the *Ewart Park* phase from the term used to describe its characteristic sword, but its industries are often discussed on a regional basis, when regional terms are used: *Llantwit* for Wales, from a find near Cardiff; *Stogursey*, from a north Somerset find, for the south-west; and *Carp's Tongue* for the south-east and East Anglia. The Carp's Tongue material presents a particular problem and is discussed separately.

Ewart Park swords were the basic edged weapon of the period, with their typically straight ricassi and two or three rivet holes in the hilt (fig. 18). The bulk of the finds is from the south-east. Spearheads, on the other hand, appear everywhere (fig. 18), in a variety of blade shapes and with peg holes. Shafts were sometimes fitted with bulb-ended ferrules (fig. 18).

The enormous development of socketed axes, both in numbers and in types, is a keynote of the time. The variety of socketed axe types has always made them difficult to discuss. The bronzesmiths plainly had a repertoire of *shapes*, with their own chronologies and industrial links, and a repertoire of *decorations* for both body and mouth, also with their own histories, and these they constantly intermingled so that a general typological sequence is extremely difficult to perceive. The basic forms probably originated within the Wilburton tradition.

Small socketed axes with mouth mouldings appeared in the Isle of Harty find, which probably stands near the beginning of the phase, together with bronze moulds for their manufacture (plate 15). The small socketed axe from the Burton upon Stather find is broadly contemporary (fig. 19) and the Stogursey find, also early Ewart Park, had a similar axe; types like these were widespread. Bag-shaped axes (fig. 19), probably with Irish links, were also generally fairly common. Plain socketed axes, like those from Worthing, and south-eastern axes, like that from Cheddar (Somerset), also occur everywhere.

Within the socketed axes, however, some types stand out as

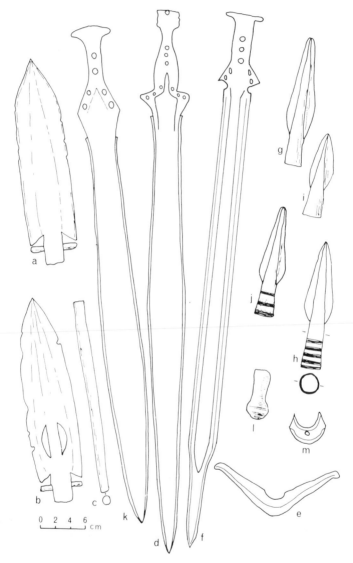

Fig. 18. a-c: Barbed spearheads, ferrule; Broadness (Kent) (after C. Burgess, D. Coombs and G. Davies). **d-e:** Hallstatt C sword, chape; Ebberston (North Yorks). **f:** Carp's Tongue sword; river Thames (both after Megaw and Simpson). **g-h:** Late pegged spearheads; Reach Fen (Cambridgeshire) (*Inv. Arch.* GB 17). **i-j:** Late pegged spearheads; Watford (Hertfordshire) (after Coombs). **k:** Ewart Park sword; Northumberland (after Megaw and Simpson). **l:** Bulb-ended ferrule; Croydon (London) (*Inv. Arch.* GB 39). **m:** Chape; Levington (Suffolk) (after Megaw and Simpson).

Plate 15. Part of a find from Isle of Harty (Kent). *Above:* Lugged chisels (length of longest 170 mm, 6⅝ inches), reel-shaped toggle, waster from casting. *Below:* Bronze moulds for casting socketed axes and gouges, axes and gouges cast in these moulds and two socketed hammers (Ashmolean Museum).

specialities of the various regions. The manufacture of varieties of faceted axe was concentrated in East Anglia and the Middle Fens, like that from Feltwell Fen (fig. 19), inspired by a north European form. A type of relatively heavy socketed axe with a single mouth moulding and three-rib decorative motif appears concentrated in South Wales although its manufacture was widespread, judging by the finds of moulds from Cornwall, Wessex and the Thames valley. The moulds are all of stone, suggesting that they represent a particular manufacturing tradition, probably with south-western links. This has been called the Bulford-Helsbury tradition, after the mould finds from Wiltshire and Cornwall, and the axes, which appear in the Llantwit (fig. 19) and Stogursey finds, used to be called South Welsh axes but are now named the Stogursey type. A different kind of ribbed axe is typical of Yorkshire and is called the Yorkshire type (fig. 19). One of these also appeared at Stogursey, demonstrating the degree of interchange across Britain.

A range of basic tools seems to have been available every-where, although much of the surviving material comes from eastern Britain. These included a variety of socketed knives and some tanged forms (fig. 20), socketed gouges (plate 15 and fig. 20), carpenters' chisels, like that from Watford (fig. 20), and simpler tanged chisels. Also available were light socketed hammers, occasional saws, awls, punches and socketed sickles. The Isle of Harty find gives a good idea of the tool kit (plate 15). Narrow-bladed palstaves, too, often occur in the large finds; they may still have been in use, or even perhaps in manufacture, or they may have been simply old scrap. Most of the tools were developments from Wilburton types, on the basis of still older ideas.

To judge by the fragments which appear in many Ewart Park finds, sheet metal vessels continued to be used and made, although the way in which many of them were patched shows that they could last a long time. Cauldrons, like the example with a corrugated neck from the Thames at Battersea, often come from watery contexts and could have been votive offerings (plate 16). Buckets sometimes come from occupation sites, like those from South Cadbury or Heathery Burn Cave (fig. 21), although no context is known for the fine example from Nannau, which has the earlier form of base plate.

Bun-shaped ingots (fig. 22) and fragments of such ingots seem to be normal elements in the large finds, although the evidence survives better in the south-east. Analysis has shown that these are usually fairly pure copper, much of which came from the Alpine area via northern France and from Brittany, although in western Britain the exploitation of indigenous copper sources was increasing. The bun ingots are the result of smelting ore in a bowl furnace although the large ingots may be the product of more than one smelt. Elaborate bronze bivalve socketed axe and tool moulds were in common use, like that from Southall (London) (fig. 22 and plate 15), and they were themselves, presumably, made in clay moulds. Swords and spears seem to have been cast directly in clay moulds. Scrap metal, damaged pieces and wasters from casting (fig. 22 and plate 15) often make up the bulk of the material in the group finds, which are best regarded as smith's caches and workshops, in effect as little bronze foundries.

Gold ornaments stand apart from the Ewart Park finds; they usually occur in gold hoards or as single pieces, sometimes from occupation sites. Gold armrings, some fairly simple and solid,

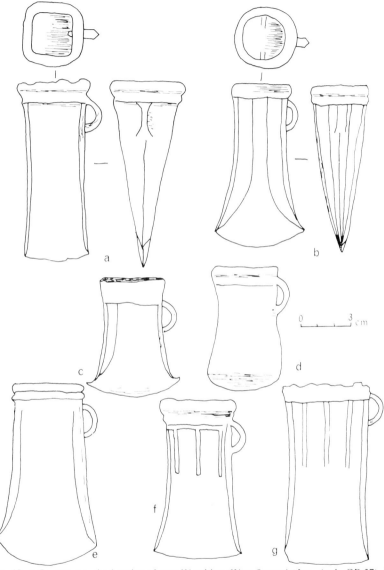

Fig. 19. a: Square-mouthed socketed axe; Worthing (West Sussex) (*Inv. Arch.* GB 37). **b:** Faceted socketed axe; Feltwell Fen (Norfolk) (*Inv. Arch.* GB 35). **c:** Small socketed axe; Burton upon Stather (Humberside) (*Inv. Arch.* GB 23). **d:** Bag-shaped axe; East Hemsworth (Dorset). **e:** South-eastern axe; Cheddar (Somerset) (both after Pearce). **f:** Yorkshire socketed axe; Everthorpe (Humberside) (after Langmaid). **g:** Stogursey or South Welsh socketed axe; Llantwit (South Glamorgan) (after Grimes).

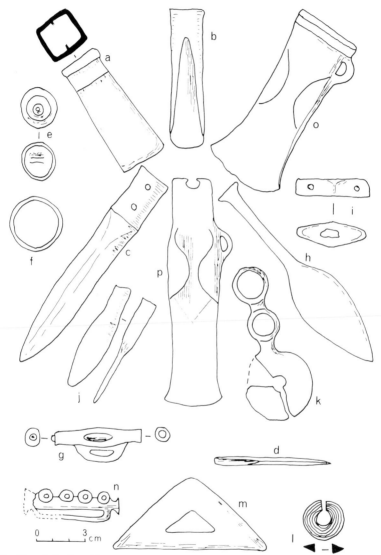

Fig. 20. a-d: Socketed hammer, socketed gouge, socketed knife, awl; Thorndon (Suffolk) (*Inv. Arch.* GB 11). **e-i:** Circular button, ring, 'bugle-shaped' object, tanged knife, cap mounting; Reach Fen (Cambridgeshire). (*Inv. Arch.* GB 17). **j-k:** Socketed mortising chisel, razor; Watford (Hertfordshire) (after Coombs). **l:** Gold 'lockring'; Castle Cary (Somerset) (after Pearce). **m:** Hog-back blade; Eaton (Norfolk). **n:** 'Slide'; river Thames (both after Megaw and Simpson). **o:** Wing-decorated axe; Worthing (West Sussex) (*Inv. Arch.* GB 37). **p:** Winged axe; Beachy Head (East Sussex) (*Inv. Arch.* GB 40).

others made from sheet gold with elaborate cup-shaped terminals and sometimes decorated, have been found in hoards at Morvah (Cornwall) and Caister-on-Sea (Norfolk) (plate 17). Penannular 'lock-rings' and 'dress fasteners' (a little like modern cufflinks, but with a solid bar instead of a chain) are also occasional finds. Much of this goldwork came from Ireland ready-made, but some may have been made up in Britain.

The Carp's Tongue complex

The Carp's Tongue complex takes its name from its character-istic sword, which is said to have a blade shaped like a carp's tongue (fig. 18), together with a T-shaped terminal and a squarish ricasso. The blade shape permits the sword to be used both as a slashing and as a thrusting weapon, probably by a cavalryman. With the sword went the new bag-shaped chapes (fig. 18) and the so-called Carp's Tongue bric-à-brac, various 'bugle-shaped' objects, studs and slides, used probably as strap fasteners for warrior equipment and horse gear (fig. 20). True winged axes, with curved flanges replacing sockets, are also a part of the complex (fig. 20).

Finds with this range of objects, like those from Addington (London) (plate 18) or Reach Fen (Cambridgeshire), often also include ingots, wing-decorated socketed axes, which occur also at Isle of Harty with a mould (plate 15), and ribbed socketed axes, tools like socketed gouges, socketed knives, tanged knives, various chisels and roughly triangular hog-back knives. Pegged spearheads with bands of decoration around the socket are also characteristic. The extent to which much of this material can be separated from the usual run of southern British Ewart Park metalwork into a specific Carp's Tongue group is debatable.

In Britain all this material appears principally in the south-east, with concentrations in the Thames valley and along the coast. This matches the very large quantities of similar material in north-west France. Brittany alone has produced over fifty relevant finds, and it looks as if the development of the complex was centred here, where smiths could draw upon late Urnfield ideas to produce the typical sword, although some types, like the wing-decorated axes, may have been British models.

However, only three complete Carp's Tongue swords have been found in Britain; the bulk of the material comes from founders' caches and consists of broken fragments waiting to be melted down. This seems to rule out the idea that the swords came in the hands of invading north French warriors, and it

Plate 16. Cauldron from the Thames at Battersea (height 410 mm, 16⅛ inches) (British Museum).

suggests that some of it, at least, may have arrived in Britain as scrap bronze together with copper bun ingots, while some of it may have been made and broken locally. Altogether, the Carp's Tongue complex underlines yet again the closeness of cross-Channel links.

The Broadward complex

The finds of this complex stand somewhat apart from contemporary Ewart Park metalwork. They occur in the Thames valley and in a broad arc from Dartmoor through the Welsh Marches, with the important find from Broadward (Hereford and Worcester), to the Humber estuary. They include a few late palstaves and Ewart Park swords, but essentially this is a spear complex.

Hollow-bladed spearheads are prominent in the finds, but most characteristic are barbed hollow-bladed spearheads, often with large peg rivets which extend beyond the barbs, rendering the spears useless for practical purposes and indicating their ceremonial nature (fig. 18). A few of the barbed spearheads have lunate blade openings like that from Broadness (Kent) (fig. 18), and

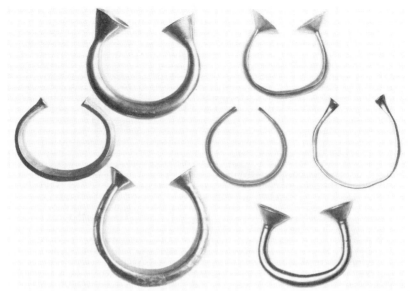

Plate 17. Gold penannular armrings. The three on the left from Morvah (Cornwall), found with three others (diameter of largest 87 mm, 3⅜ inches) (British Museum); the four on the right from Caister-on-Sea (Norfolk) (Castle Museum, Norwich).

Plate 18. Find from Addington (London). *Left:* Pieces of bun ingot. *Right:* Fragments of plain, ribbed and wing-decorated axe, winged axe, gouge, ? scabbard mounting, plain socketed axe, upper part of Carp's Tongue sword (length 44 mm, 1¾ inches) (British Museum).

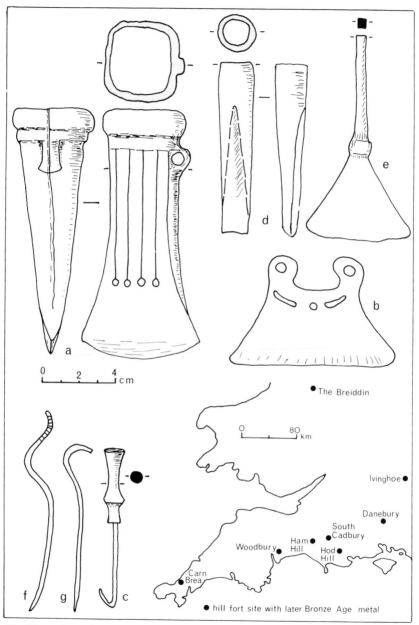

Fig. 23. a-c: Sompting axe, Class 3 razor, pin (or similar object); Danebury (Hampshire) (after B. Cunliffe and B. O'Connor). **d-g:** Socketed gouge, wide-bladed tanged chisel, two swan-necked pins; Ham Hill (Somerset) (after Pearce).

Plate 19. Part of a find from Llyn Fawr (Mid Glamorgan). *Left:* Cauldron. *Above:* Fragmentary Hallstatt C iron sword, iron spear, two wing-shaped cheek pieces, two rear-looped discs or phalerae (diameter 150 mm, 5⅞ inches). *Below:* Two sickles, one with iron socket, gouge, Hallstatt C razor, belt hook, ornamental plate, and two axes (National Museum of Wales).

they often come from watery contexts. In Britain, the finds are concentrated heavily in the Thames valley, with a scatter up the east coast. Native smiths soon produced local versions with some Ewart Park features, known as Thames and Holme Pierrepoint swords. All these swords usually occur as single finds. Other Hallstatt C elements are more widely scattered in Britain and are sometimes found with ordinary native material, often on settlement sites. These include harness fittings and ornamental jangles like those from Parc-y-meirch (Clwyd), elaborate Class 3 razors like those from occupation at Danebury and Ham Hill, chunky neckrings and armrings, and probably the earliest swan-necked pins (fig. 23).

At the same time the Armorican axes appear — slender, socketed pieces with simple rib decoration. These axes usually have a high lead content. They are found in quantity in Brittany, and to an extent in southern Britain. Closely related to these Armorican axes are those with a variety of rib and pellet decorations, often with a very high tin content, like the hoard from Eggardon (Dorset). Linked with both these are the

Sompting axes, named from a Sussex find, with their distinctive back-to-front sockets. These usually occur in single-type hoards, but there was one from Danebury (fig. 23). Probably contemporary are finds like that from Gwinear (Cornwall) of over fifty square-socketed axes, found in a pit, packed together. Some of these axes presumably served the usual utilitarian functions. Others, like the high tin group, may have been essentially axe ingots and demonstrate the increased exploitation of south-western and Breton ores.

The handful of associated finds shows that these axes and the Hallstatt C bronzes represent the final smithing traditions of the bronze age. The Sompting hoard itself contained an iron lump. The 'wet-site' deposit from Llyn Fawr (Mid Glamorgan) had two cauldrons, Hallstatt C razors and horse gear, an iron Hallstatt C sword, two native bronze sickles and a careful copy in iron, and an iron spearhead of Hallstatt C type (plate 19).

Bronze in society, 900 to 600 BC

Why did the late bronze age communities produce so much bronzework, and why did its production cease so suddenly? It seems that the quantity of metal and the greatly increased range of types must reflect a new prosperity, related to population growth and improved land exploitation, but requiring a higher degree of social organisation, which probably involved a sharper division into rulers and ruled. The swords and related horsy gear and the gold ornaments look like the accoutrements of the nobly born, the spears conceivably belonged to free warriors, and the axes and tools were the equipment of peasants more or less bound to the soil; certainly these distinctions had developed by the time the iron age was under way.

A number of hilltops later occupied by hillforts, like Ivinghoe Beacon (Buckinghamshire) or the Breiddin (Powys), have produced occupation material linked with Ewart Park bronzes (fig. 23). These may have been the seats of noble families who co-operated to organise the cross-Channel metal exchange, which may even have ramified down the Atlantic coast, controlled the smiths and their foundries and managed the distribution of bronzes, and who were supported by tribute of produce and labour from the countryside which they controlled.

In the Llyn Fawr-Hallstatt C phase all these tendencies are increasingly obvious. Hillfort sites like South Cadbury, Ham Hill and Danebury were occupied, many of them probably with their own bronzesmiths, and a string of coastal sites, like Mount Batten

(Devon), Weymouth Bay (Dorset) and probably some of the Thames-side settlements, were points where raw metal was received and made up. The Hallstatt C metalwork in Britain probably arrived through the usual exchange networks, but conceivably the swords point to raiding parties; if so, then this will have encouraged the authority of local rulers.

With the Hallstatt bronze, however, came iron and, perhaps, some blacksmiths. The rapid dissemination of ironworking must have had a shattering effect upon British bronzesmiths; it must explain the few bronze socketed axe types from the final period, and perhaps the great mass of Ewart Park finds and some of the latest axe hoards, buried after the bronze market collapsed in the hope that business would improve. This proved vain, and bronze was never again used for normal tools and weapons. Nevertheless, bronze age developments were crucial. By its end, society in southern Britain was hierarchical, largely sedentary and peasant-based, and so it was to remain, modified but essentially unaltered, until the industrial revolution. It is these processes which the metalwork helps us to understand.

6
Further reading

Barrett, J., and Bradley, R. *The British Later Bronze Age.* British Archaeological Reports, 83, i, ii, 1980.

Burgess, C. *The Age of Stonehenge.* London, 1980.

Burgess, C., and Coombs, D. *Bronze Age Hoards : Some Finds Old and New.* British Archaeological Reports, 67, 1979.

Coles, J. M., and Harding, A. F. *The Bronze Age in Europe.* London, 1979.

Inv. Arch. Inventaria Archaeologica. Publications of bronze age finds through the International Congress of Prehistoric and Protohistoric Sciences, 1955 continuing.

Lynch, F., and Burgess, C. *Prehistoric Man in Wales and the West.* Bath, 1972.

Megaw, V., and Simpson, D. *Introduction to British Prehistory.* Leicester, 1979.

Pearce, S. *The Bronze Age Metalwork of South-western Britain.* British Archaeological Reports, 120, i, ii, 1983.

Rowlands, M. *The Organization of Middle Bronze Age Metalworking.* British Archaeological Reports, 31, 1976.

Wainwright, G. *Mount Pleasant, Dorset.* London, 1979.

Index

Note: illustrated finds are not included here and should be found in the lists of illustrations and captions.